FRENCH

to go

A weekend's worth of **essential** words and phrases

Translated by Athene Chanter

Michael O'Mara Books Limited

First published in Great Britain in 2014 by
Michael O'Mara Books Limited
9 Lion Yard
Tremadoc Road
London SW4 7NQ

A CIP catalogue record for this book is available from the
British Library.

Papers used by Michael O'Mara Books Limited are natural,
recyclable products made from wood grown in sustainable
forests. The manufacturing processes conform to the
environmental regulations of the country of origin.

ISBN: 978-1-78243-209-8 in paperback print format

1 2 3 4 5 6 7 8 9 10

Designed and typeset by Claire Cater

Printed and bound by CPI Group (UK) Ltd, Croydon, CR0 4YY

www.mombooks.com

CONTENTS

INTRODUCTION

Concise yet informative, *French to go* is
ideal for weekend visits to *la belle France* –
a regular glance at the contents of this
pocket-sized book will ensure you'll never
be lost for words.

Clear and precise, the pronunciation that
follows each French word and phrase has
been devised to simplify the French language
for the English-speaking user, with the aim
of producing more relaxed and flowing
conversations with the people you meet.

Make the most of your French adventure
with *French to go* – whether you're making
a hotel reservation, finding your way to the
beach or chatting up the locals, speaking
French has never been easier.

NOTE ON PHONETIC PRONUNCIATION:

When you see a 'ñ', you should nasalize the vowel before it and not pronounce the 'n' itself. For example, 'man' would be pronounced as in the familiar French word 'fin', rather than the English 'man'. All nouns in French are preceded by a masculine or feminine article. When you see a noun with an alternative ending in brackets, this indicates the feminine or plural of the word. Nouns in the vocabulary section also carry their gender articles.

THE BASICS

Hi
Salut
sa'loo

Goodbye
Au revoir
oh ruh'vwar

Hello / Good morning
Bonjour
boñ'zhoor

Good afternoon
Bon après-midi
bon ap'ray mee'dee

Good evening
Bonsoir
boñ'swar

Good night
Bonne nuit
bon nwee

Yes
Oui
wee

No
Non
noñ

Please
S'il vous plaît
seel voo play

Thank you
Merci
mair'see

Thank you very much
Merci beaucoup
mair'see boh'koo

You're welcome.
Je vous en prie / Je t'en prie.
zhuh vooz oñ pree / zhuh toñ pree

How are you?
**Comment allez
   -vous? / Ça va?**
*ko'moñ ta'lay
   voo / sa va*

Fine / not bad
Bien / pas mal

byañ / pah mal

Pleased to meet you.
**Je suis hereux(se) de faire votre /
   ta connaissance.**
*zhuh sweez uhr'ruh(ruhze) duh fair votr /
   ta kon'ay'soñs*

Excuse me
Excusez-moi
eks'koo'zay mwa

Sorry
Désolé(e)
day'zo'lay

Pardon?
Pardon?
par'doñ

Do you speak English?
Parlez-vous anglais?
par'lay vooz oñ'glay

I speak some French.
Je parle un peu français.
zhuh parl uñ puh froñ'say

I don't understand.
Je ne comprends pas.
zhuh nuh koñ'proñ pah

I'm English
Je suis anglais(e)
zhuh sweez oñ'glay / (glayz)

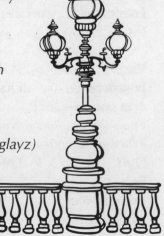

9

My name is …
Je m'appelle …
zhuh ma'pel

Could you repeat that more slowly, please?
**Est-ce que vous pourriez répéter cela plus
    lentement s'il vous plait?**
*ess kuh voo poo'ree'ay ray'pay'tay suh'la ploo
    loñ'tuh'moñ seel voo play*

Could I pass by?
Est-ce que je pourrais passer?
ess kuh zhuh poo'ray pass'ay

Why?	What?
Pourquoi?	**Quoi?**
poor'kwa	*kwa*

Who?	When?
Qui?	**Quand?**
kee	*koñ*

How? | How much / How many?
Comment? | **Combien?**
ko'moñ | *kom'byañ*

Where? | Which?
Où? | **Lequel?**
oo | *luh'kel*

Is it far?
Est-ce que c'est loin?
ess kuh say lwañ

Could I have … ?
Est-ce que je pourrais avoir … ?
ess kuh zhuh poo'rayz a'vwar

Can you tell me … ?
Est-ce que vous pouvez me dire … ?
ess kuh voo poo'vay muh deer

Can you help me?
Pouvez-vous m'aider?
poo'vay voo may'day

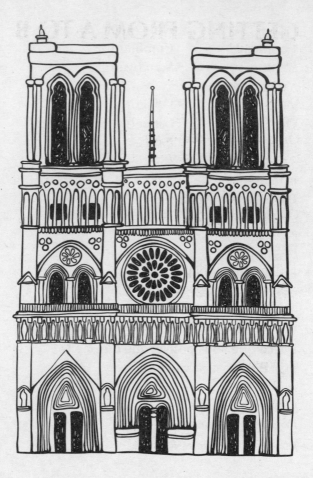

2 GETTING FROM A TO B

AIRPORTS

Where do I check in?
Où est l'enregistrement?
oo ay loñ'rezh'eestr'moñ

Where is / Where are the … ?
Où est / Où sont les … ?
oo ay / oo soñ

departure lounge
la salle d'embarquement
la sal doñ'bar'kuh'moñ

gate
la porte
la port

baggage reclaim
la réception des bagages
la ray'seps'yoñ day ba'gazh

luggage trolleys
les chariots à bagages
lay sha'ree'oh a bag'azh

help / information desk
le bureau d'information
luh boo'roh dañ'for'mas'yoñ

ladies' / gents' toilets
les toilettes pour femmes / hommes
lay twa'let poor fam / om

Which terminal does my plane leave from?
De quel terminal part mon vol?
duh kel ter'mee'nal par mon vol

My suitcase has been damaged.
Ma valise a été endommagée.
ma va'leez a ay'tay on'dom'azh'ay

Are there any cash machines here?
Y a-t-il des distributeurs de monnaie ici?
*ee a teel day dees'tree'boo'tuhr duh mo'nay
ee'see?*

Is there a bureau de change nearby?
Y a-t-il un bureau de change par ici?
ee a teel uñ boo'roh duh shoñzh par ee'see

Is there a bus / train to the town centre?
**Y a-t-il un bus / train pour aller au centre
ville?**
*ee a teel uñ boos / trañ poor a'lay oh soñtr
veel*

TAXI!

Is there a taxi rank nearby?
Y a-t-il une station de taxis par ici?
ee a teel oon stas'yoñ duh tak'see par ee'see

Could I book a taxi for … ?
Est-ce que je pourrais réserver un taxi pour … ?
*ess kuh zhuh poo'ray ray'zair'vay uñ tak'see
  poor*

How much will it cost to get to … ?
Combien cela va coûter pour aller jusqu'à … ?
*kom'byañ suh'la va koo'tay poor a'lay
  zhoos'ka*

Take me to this address, please.
Emmenez-moi à cette adresse, s'il vous plaît.
eh'muh'nay mwa a set a'dress, seel voo play

PUBLIC TRANSPORT

I'd like a single / return to …
**Je voudrais un aller simple /
  aller retour pour …**
*zhuh voo'drayz uñ a'lay sañ'pl /
  a'lay ruh'toor poor*

What time does the next train / bus to …
  leave?
**A quelle heure part le prochain train / bus
  pour … ?**
a kel uhr par luh pro'shañ trañ / boos poor

How long does it take to get to … ?
**Combien de temps cela prend pour
  aller à … ?**
kom'byañ duh toñ suh'la proñ poor a'lay a

Does this bus / train / tram go to … ?
Est-ce que ce bus / train / tram va à … ?
ess kuh suh boos / trañ / tram va a

Which platform does it leave from?
Il part de quel quai?
eel par duh kel kay

POSSIBLE REPLY
Your train leaves from platform number …
Votre train part du quai numéro …
votr trañ par doo kay noo'may'roh

Which bus goes to … ?
Quel bus va à … ?
kel boos va a

POSSIBLE REPLY
You'll need bus number … for …
Il faut prendre le bus numéro … pour …
eel foh proñdr luh boos noo'may'roh …
poor …

Where should I catch the number … bus?

**Où est-ce que je peux prendre le bus
numéro … ?**

*oo ess kuh zhuh puh proñdr luh boos
noo'may'roh*

Do I have to change bus / train?

Est-ce que je dois changer de bus / train?

ess kuh zhuh dwa shonzh'ay duh bus / trañ

How much is the fare to … ?

Combien coûte le ticket pour … ?

kom'byañ koot luh tee'kay poor

What time is the last bus / train to … ?

**A quelle heure passe le dernier bus /
train pour … ?**

a kel uhr pass luh dairn'yay boos / trañ poor

What is the next stop?

Quel est le prochain arrêt?

kel ay luh pro'shen a'ray

Please tell me when we get to …
**S'il vous plaît, est-ce que vous pourrez me
    dire quand nous serons à …**
*seel voo play ess kuh voo poo'ray muh deer
    koñ noo suh'roñ a*

Is this seat free?
Est-ce que ce siège est libre?
ess kuh suh see'ezh ay leebr

Do you have any left luggage lockers?
Est-ce que vous avez une consigne ici?
ess kuh vooz a'vay oon koñ'seen'yuh ee'see

CAR & BICYCLE HIRE

Where can I hire a car / bicycle?
**Où est-ce que je peux louer une voiture /
    un vélo?**
*oo ess kuh zhuh puh loo'ay oon vwa'toor /
    uñ vay'lo*

I'd like to hire a car for a day / week.

Je voudrais louer une voiture pour une journée / semaine.

zhuh voo'dray loo'ay oon vwa'toor poor oon zhoor'nay / suh'men

What is the daily / weekly rate?

Quel est le tarif par jour / par semaine?

kel ay luh ta'reef par zhoor / par suh'men

POSSIBLE REPLY

It will cost … euros per day / per week.

Cela vous coûtera … euros par jour / par semaine.

suh'la voo koot'ra … uh'roh par zhoor / par suh'men

Can I park here? / Where can I park?
Est-ce que je peux me garer ici? / Où y a-t-il un parking?
ess kuh zhuh puh muh ga'ray ee'see / oo ee a teel oon par'keeng

Where can I buy petrol?
Où y a-t-il une station d'essence?
oo ee a teel oon stas'yoñ dess'oñse

Does the car take unleaded or diesel?
Est-ce que la voiture utilise du diesel ou de l'essence?
ess kuh la vwa'toor oo'tee'leez doo dee'sel oo duh less'oñse

Can I leave my bike here?
Est-ce que je peux laisser mon vélo ici?
ess kuh zhuh puh less'ay mon vay'lo ee'see

Is there a bike shop nearby?
Y a-t-il un magasin de vélo par ici?
ee a teel uñ ma'ga'zañ duh vay'lo par ee'see

BY SEA

Where do I catch the ferry to … ?

**Où est-ce que je peux prendre le ferry
    pour … ?**

oo ess kuh zhuh puh proñdr luh feh'ree poor

When does the next ferry / boat leave for … ?

**A quelle heure part le prochain ferry /
    bateau pour … ?**

a kel uhr par luh pro'shañ feh'ree / ba'toh poor

POSSIBLE REPLIES

It costs …

Cela coûte …

suh'la koot

It's …

C'est …

say

on the left / right
à gauche / à droite
a gohsh / a drwat

straight ahead
droit devant / tout droit
drwa duh'voñ / too drwa

behind / in front of
derrière / devant
derry'air / duh'voñ

near / next to / opposite
près de / à coté de / en face de
pray duh / a kot'ay duh / oñ fass duh

over there
par là
par la

up / down the stairs
en haut / en bas des escaliers
oñ oh / oñ bah dayz es'kal'yay

Follow the signs above.
Suivez les panneaux.
swee'vay lay pan'oh

There's a train to … at …
Il y a un train pour … à … heures.
eel ee a uñ trañ poor … a … uhr

Yes, you must change at …
Oui, il faut que vous changiez à …
wee eel foh kuh voo shoñ'zhee'ay a

The next boat for … will leave at …
Le prochain bâteau pour … part à … heures.
luh pro'shañ ba'toh poor … par a … uhr

3 BED & BREAKFAST

HOTELS & HOSTELS

Do you have any vacancies?
Est-ce que vous avez des chambres libres?
ess kuh vooz a'vay day shoñbr leebr

I would like …
Je voudrais …
zhuh voo'dray

   a room with a good view
   une chambre avec vue
   oon shoñbr a'vek voo

I reserved a single room / double room …
J'ai réservé une chambre simple / double …
zhay ray'zair'vay oon shoñbr sañ'pl / doo'bl

with twin beds
avec deux lits
a'vek duh lee

with a double bed
avec un lit double
a'vek uñ lee doo'bl

with a shower and toilet
avec une douche et des toilettes
a'vek oon doosh ay day twa'let

with a bath
avec une baignoire
a'vek oon ben'war

a balcony
un balcon
uñ bal'coñ

How much is … ?
Combien coûte(nt) … ?
kom'byañ koot

bed and breakfast …
la chambre et le petit déjeuner …
la shoñbr ay luh puh'tee day'zhuh'nay

half-board …
la demi-pension …
la duh'mee poñ'syoñ

full-board …
la pension complète
la poñ'syoñ kom'plet

… per night
… par nuit
par nwee

… per week
… par semaine
par suh'men

Is breakfast included?
Est-ce que le petit déjeuner est compris?
ess kuh luh puh'tee day'zhuh'nay ay
    com'pree

I'd like to stay for …
Je voudrais rester pour …
zhuh voo'dray res'tay poor

one night / two nights
une nuit / deux nuits
oon nwee / duh nwee

a week / two weeks
une semaine / deux semaines
oon suh'men / duh suh'men

Is there a reduction for children?
Y a-t-il un tarif réduit pour les enfants?
ee a teel uñ ta'reef ray'dwee poor layz oñ'foñ

POSSIBLE REPLIES

It's half-price for children.
C'est demi-tarif pour les enfants.
say duh'mee ta'reef poor layz oñ'foñ

There are no discounts for children.
Il n'y a pas de réductions pour les enfants.
eel nee a pa duh ray'dooks'yoñ poor layz oñ'foñ

Does the room have … ?
Est-ce que la chambre a … ?
ess kuh la shoñbr a

a radio / a television
une radio / une télévision
oon rad'yoh / tay'lay'veez'yoñ

room service
service d'étage
sair'vees day'tazh

a minibar
un minibar
uñ mee'nee'bar

air-conditioning
la climatisation
la klee'ma'tee'zas'yoñ

a hairdryer
un sèche-cheveux
uñ sesh shuh'vuh

Wi-Fi
Wi-Fi
wee fee

a Wi-Fi code
un mot de passe Wi-Fi
uñ moh duh pass wee'fee

a safe
un coffre-fort
uñ koffr for

Do you have any cheaper rooms?
Avez-vous des chambres moins chères?
a'vay voo day shoñbr mwañ shair

> **POSSIBLE REPLY**
> This is our cheapest room.
> **Voici notre chambre la moins chère.**
> *vwa'see notr shoñbr la mwañ shair*

Do you allow pets in the rooms?
Est-ce que les animaux sont autorisés dans les chambres?
ess kuh layz a'nee'moh soñ oh'toh'ree'zay doñ lay shoñbr

Is there a night porter on duty?
Y a-t-il un portier de nuit en service?
ee a teel uñ port'yay duh nwee oñ sair'vees

Can I have a wake-up call at … ?

Pouvez-vous me réveiller par téléphone à … heures?

poo'vay voo muh ray'vay'ay par tay'lay'fon a … uhr

I like to stay out late, so will I need a key?

J'aime rester dehors tard, alors est-ce que j'ai besoin d'une clé?

zhem res'tay duh'or tar a'lor ess kuh zhay buhz'wañ doon klay

I'd like breakfast in my room tomorrow.

Je voudrais prendre mon petit-déjeuner dans ma chambre demain.

zhuh voo'dray proñdr moñ puh'tee day'zhuh'nay doñ ma shoñbr duh'mañ

What time is breakfast / dinner served?

A quelle heure est servi le petit-déjeuner / le dîner?

a kel uhr ay sair'vee luh puh'tee day'zhuh'nay / luh dee'nay

I'd like to make a complaint.
Je voudrais faire une réclamation.
zhuh voo'dray fair oon ray'kla'mas'yoñ

The room is too cold / hot / small / dirty / noisy.
**La chambre est trop froide / chaude / petite /
sale / bruyante**
*la shoñbr ay troh frwad / shohd / puh'teet /
sal / broo'yoñt*

Could I have some clean towels, please?
**Est-ce que je peux avoir des serviettes
propres, s'il vous plaît?**
*ess kuh zhuh puhz a'vwar day sair'vyet propr
seel voo play*

The shower doesn't work.
La douche ne marche pas.
la doosh nuh marsh pah

I'm not satisfied.
Je ne suis pas satisfé(e).
zhuh nuh swee pah sa'tees'fay

I'd like another room, please.
Je voudrais une autre chambre, s'il vous plaît.
zhuh voo'drayz oon otr shoñbr seel voo play

Can you recommend any good bars /
restaurants / night clubs?
**Pouvez-vous me recommander des bars /
des restaurants / des boîtes de nuit
sympathiques?**
*poo'vay voo muh ruh'ko'moñ'day day bar /
day res'toh'roñ / day bwat duh nwee
sam'pa'teek*

Are there any areas I should avoid at night?
**Y a-t-il des quartiers que je devrais éviter
la nuit?**
*ee a teel day kart'yay kuh zhuh duh'vrayz ay'
vee'tay la nwee*

I'd like to make a phone call.
Je voudrais passer un coup de fil.
zhuh voo'dray pass'ay uñ kood feel

Do you know where I can print out my
  boarding pass?
**Savez-vous où je pourrais imprimer ma carte
  d'embarquement?**
*sa'vay voo oo zhuh poo'rayz am'pree'may
  ma kart dom'barkuh'moñ*

What time is check out?
Il faut libérer la chambre à quelle heure?
eel foh lee'bay'ray la shoñbr a kel uhr

Can I leave my luggage in reception?
**Est-ce que je peux laisser mes bagages à la
  réception?**
*ess kuh zhuh puh less'ay may bag'azh a la
  ray'seps'yoñ*

Can I have the bill?
Est-ce que je peux avoir l'addition?
ess kuh zhuh puhz a'vwar la'dees'yoñ

CAMPING

Where's the nearest campsite?
Où est le camping le plus proche?
oo ay luh kom'peeng luh ploo prosh

May we camp here?
Pouvons-nous camper ici?
poo'voñ noo kom'pay ee'see

How much to stay here … ?
Combien cela coûterait-t-il de rester ici … ?
*kom'byañ suh'la koot'ray teel duh res'tay
  ee'see*

per day	per person
par jour	**par personne**
par zhoor	*par pair'son*

per car
par voiture
par vwa'toor

per tent | per caravan
par tente | **par caravane**
par toñt | *par caravan*

Where are the toilets / the showers?
Où sont les toilettes / les douches?
oo soñ lay twa'let / lay doosh

Is there / are there … ?
Y a-t-il … ?
ee a teel

public telephones
des téléphones publiques
day tay'lay'fon poo'bleek

local shops
des magasins de quartier
day ma'ga'zañ duh karty'ay

a swimming pool
une piscine
oon pee'seen

an electricity supply
une prise électrique
oon preez ay'lek'treek

places to eat nearby
des endroits pour manger près d'ici
dayz on'drwa poor moñ'zhay pray dee'see

Can we cook here?
Est-ce que nous pouvons cuisiner ici?
ess kuh noo poo'voñ kwee'zee'nay ee'see

Do you allow barbecues?
Est-ce que les barbecues sont permis ici?
ess kuh lay bar'buh'kyoo son pair'mee ee'see

Where's the nearest beach?
Où est la plage la plus proche?
oo ay la plazh la ploo prosh

POSSIBLE REPLIES

We have no vacancies at the moment.
C'est complet en ce moment.
say kom'play oñ suh mo'moñ

Our prices are …
Nos tarifs sont …
noh ta'reef soñ

I can recommend another hotel nearby.
Je peux vous recommander un autre hotel près d'ici.
zhuh puh voo ruh'ko'moñ'day uñ otr o'tel pray dee'see

How long do you want to stay?
Combien de temps voulez-vous rester?
kom'byañ duh toñ voo'lay voo res'tay

That'll be … euros.
Cela fera … euros.
suh'la fuh'ra … uh'roh

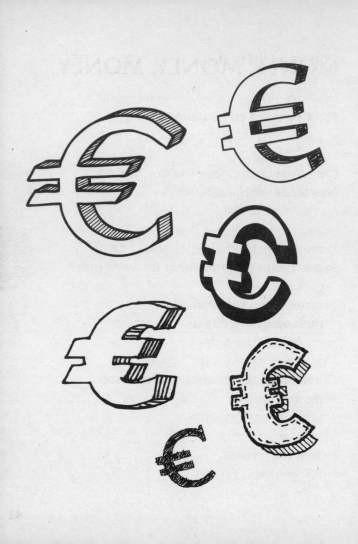

4 MONEY, MONEY, MONEY

GETTING IT

Where can I find … ?
Où est-ce que je peux trouver … ?
oo ess kuh zhuh puh troo'vay

a bank
une banque
oon boñk

a currency exchange office
un bureau de change
uñ boo'roh duh shoñzh

a cash machine
un distributeur
uñ dees'tree'boo'tuhr

What's the current exchange rate?
Quel est le taux de change actuel?
kel ay luh toh duh shoñzh ak'too'el

How much commission do you charge?
A combien s'élève la commission?
a kom'byañ say'lev la ko'mees'yoñ

I'd like to exchange these traveller's cheques /
   pounds for euros.
**Je voudrais échanger ces chèques de voyage /
   livres contre des euros.**
*zhuh voo'drayz ay'shoñ'zhay say shek duh
   vwa'yazh / leevr koñtr dayz uh'roh*

SPENDING IT

How much is it?
C'est combien?
say kom'byañ

Can I pay by credit card / cash?
**Est-ce que je peux payer par carte de crédit /
espèces?**
*ess kuh zhuh puh pay'ay par kart duh
kray'dee / es'pess*

Do you accept traveller's cheques?
Acceptez-vous les chèques de voyage?
ak'sep'tay voo lay shek duh vwa'yazh

5 FOOD, GLORIOUS FOOD

EATING OUT

Waiter / Waitress!
Serveur / Serveuse!
sair'vuhr / sair'vuhz

I'd like a table for one person / two people.
**Je voudrais une table pour une personne /
deux personnes.**
*zhuh voo'drayz oon tabl poor oon pair'son /
duh pair'son*

Could we have a table ... ?
Pourrions-nous avoir une table ... ?
poo'ree'oñ nooz a'vwar oon tabl

in the corner
dans le coin
doñ luh kwañ

by the window
à côté de la fenêtre
a ko'tay duh la fuh'netr

outside
dehors
duh'or

on the terrace
sur la terrasse
sur la teh'ras

Could we see the drinks / food menu?
**Pourrions-nous avoir la carte des boissons /
le menu?**
*poo'ree'oñ noo a'vwar la kart day bwa'soñ /
luh muh'noo*

We are ready to order.
Nous sommes prêts à commander.
noo som pret a ko'moñ'day

Could we have a couple more minutes to
decide, please?
**Est-ce que nous pourrions avoir plus de
temps, s'il vous plaît?**
*ess kuh noo poo'ree'oñ a'vwar ploo duh toñ
seel voo play*

I'd like to order some drinks, please.
**Je voudrais commander des boissons, s'îl
vous plait.**
*zhuh voo'dray ko'moñ'day day bwa'soñ seel
voo play*

I'd like …
Je voudrais …
zhuh voo'dray

a bottle of …
une bouteille de …
oon boo'tay duh

a glass / two glasses of …
un verre / deux verres de …
uñ vair / duh vair duh

a red / white wine
un vin rouge / blanc
uñ vañ roozh / bloñ

a sparkling / still mineral water
de l'eau gazeuse / minérale
duh loh gaz'uhz / mee'nay'ral

a beer
une bière
oon byair

a lager
une bière blonde
oon byair blond

a cider
un cidre
uñ see'dr

a gin and tonic
un gin tonic
uñ jin to'neek

a lemonade
une limonade
oon lee'mon'ard

a cola
un coca
uñ ko'ka

an orange juice
un jus d'orange
uñ zhoo do'ronzh

an apple juice
un jus de pomme
uñ zhoo duh pom

Do you have a children's menu?
Avez-vous un menu pour les enfants?
a'vay voo uñ muh'noo poor layz oñ'foñ

I'm vegetarian / vegan / coeliac. What do you recommend?
Je suis végétarien(ne) / végétalien(ne) / cœliaque. Qu'est-ce que vous me recommandez?
zhuh swee vay'zhay'tar'yan(yen) / vay'zhay'tal' yan(yen) / suhl'yak. Kess kuh voo muh ruh' ko'moñ'day

Does this dish contain nuts / wheat?
Est-ce que ce plat contient des noix / du blé?
ess kuh suh pla koñ'tyañ day nwa / doo blay

I'd like to order … followed by …
Je voudrais commander … suivi de …
zhuh voo'dray ko'moñ'day … swee'vee duh

Could I have some tomato ketchup / mustard /
   butter / olive oil / vinegar / salt / pepper,
   please?
**Je voudrais du ketchup / de la moutarde / du
   beurre / de l'huile d'olive / du vinaigre /
   du sel / du poivre, s'il vous plaît?**
*zhuh voo'dray doo ketchup / duh la moo'tard
   / doo burr / duh lweel do'leev / doo
   vee'nehgr / doo sel / doo pwavr seel
   voo play*

Could I see the dessert menu?
Est-ce que je peux voir la carte des desserts?
ess kuh zhuh puh vwar la kart day day'sair

There's been a mistake. I didn't order that (drink / meal).

Il y a une eu erreur. Je n'ai pas commandé cette boisson / ce repas.

eel ee a oo oon er'uhr. zhuh nay pah ko'moñ' day set bwa'soñ / suh ruh'pah

This knife / fork / spoon is dirty. Could I have another one?

Ce couteau / cette fourchette / cette cuillère est sale. Est-ce que je peux avoir un / une autre?

suh koo'toh / set for'shett / set kwee'yair ay sal. Ess kuh zhuh puhz a'vwar uñ / oon otr

That was delicious. Thank you.

C'était délicieux. Merci.

say'tay day'lees'yuh. mair'see

No, thank you, I'm full.

Non, merci. J'ai assez mangé.

noñ mair'see. zhay assay moñ'zhay

Can we order some coffee / tea, please?
Est-ce que nous pouvons commander du café / thé, s'il vous plaît?
ess kuh noo poo'voñ ko'moñ'day doo ka'fay / tay seel voo play

(Could we have) the bill, please?
L'addition, s'il vous plaît?
la'dees'yoñ seel voo play

Is service included?
Est-ce que le service est compris?
ess kuh luh sair'vees ay coñ'pree

POSSIBLE REPLIES

May I take your order?
Est-ce que je peux prendre votre commande?
ess kuh zhuh puh proñdr votr ko'moñ'd

I'd recommend …
Je recommande …
zhuh ruh'ko'moñd

Would you like …
Voudriez-vous …
voo'dree'ay voo

Enjoy your meal.
Bon appétit.
bon a'pay'tee

STAYING IN

grams	slices
grammes	**tranches**
gram	*troñsh*
kilograms	handfuls
kilogrammes	**poigné**
kee'lo'gram	*pwan'yay*
some	more / less
quelque(s)	**plus / moins**
kel'kuh	*ploo/mwañ*

half / quarter
demi / quart
duh'mee / kar

I'd like … grams / kilograms of …
Je voudrais … grammes / kilogrammes de …
zhuh voo'dray … gram / kee'lo'gram duh

minced meat	pork
viande hachée	**porc**
vee'oñd a'shay	*pork*
sausages	bacon
saucisses / saucissons	**bacon**
soh'sees / soh'see'soñ	*bay'kon*

flour
farine
fa'reen

How much is one-hundred grams of … ?
Combien coûte cent grammes de … ?
kom'byañ koot soñ gram duh …

I'd like a cut of the …
Je voudrais un morceau de …
zhuh voo'drayz uñ mor'soh duh

beef
bœuf
berf

(smoked) ham
jambon (fumé)
zham'boñ foo'may

(sirloin / rump / fillet / rib-eye / venison)
   steak
**(aloyau / rumsteck / filet / faux filet /
   venaison)**
*al'wa'yoh / rum'stek / fee'lay / foh fee'lay /
   vuh'nay'zoñ*

How much for …
Combien coûte …
kom'byañ koot

(smoked) fish
poisson fumé
pwa'soñ foo'may

cod
la morue
la mo'roo

haddock
l'aiglefin
lay'gluh'fañ

tuna
le thon
luh toñ

plaice
le carrelet
luh kar'lay

bass
bar
bar

perch
la perche
la persh

halibut
le flétan
luh flay'tañ

salmon
le saumon
luh so'moñ

lobster
l'homard
lom'ar

kipper
l'hareng fumé
la'roñ foo'may

shrimp
la crevette
la kruh'vet

trout
la truite
la trweet

mussles
les moules
lay mool

shellfish
les fruits de mer
lay frwee duh mair

When were these fish caught?
Quand ces poissons ont-ils été pêchés?
koñ say pwa'soñ oñ teels ay'tay pesh'ay

5

POSSIBLE REPLY
They have been freshly caught,
  sir / madam.
Ils sont frais, monsieur/madame.
eel soñ fray muh'syer / ma'dam

Where is the frozen / fridge / dairy / toiletries /
  cleaning section?
**Où se trouve le rayon des surgelés / produits
frais / produits laitiers / d'hygiène et
beauté / produits d'entretien?**
*oo suh troov luh ray'oñ day sur'zhu'lay /
prod'wee fray / prod'wee layt'yay /
dee'zhee'en ay bo'tay / prod'wee
doñ'truh'tyañ*

Where can I find … ?
Où est-ce que je peux trouver … ?
oo ess kuh zhuh puh troo'vay

Which way are the checkouts / tills?
Où sont les caisses?
oo soñ lay kess

Do you have any more of … ?
Avez-vous encore du … ?
a'vay voo oñ'kor doo

Is this item out of stock?
Est-ce que cet article est en rupture de stock?
ess kuh set ar'teekl ay oñ roop'toor duh stok

Could you recommend something similar?
Pouvez-vous me recommander un produit similaire?
poo'vay voo muh ruh'ko'moñ'day un prod'wee see'mee'lair

POSSIBLE REPLIES

It costs … euros / cents per one-hundred grams / kilograms.
Cela coûte … euros / cents les cents grammes / le kilogramme.
suh'la koot … uh'roh / soñ lay soñ gram / luh kee'lo'gram

It / they can be found on aisle number …
Vous pouvez le / les trouver dans l'allée …
voo poo'vay luh / lay troo'vay doñ la'lay

6 SIGHTS & SOUNDS

ATTRACTIONS & DIRECTIONS

Where is / Where are the … ?
Où est / où sont les … ?
oo ay / oo soñ lay

How far is the … ?
A quelle distance est le … ?
a kel dee'stoñs ay luh

I'm lost. How do I get to the … ?
**Je me suis perdu(e). Comment est-ce que je
    fais pour aller à … ?**
*zhuh muh swee pair'doo. Ko'moñ tess kuh
    zhuh fay poor a'lay a*

airport	art gallery
l'aéroport	**la gallerie d'art**
la'ay'ro'por	*la gal'ree dar*

beach **la plage** *la plazh*	bus station **la gare routière** *la gar root'yair*
castle **le château** *luh sha'toh*	cathedral **la cathédrale** *la ka'tay'dral*
cinema **le cinéma** *luh see'nay'ma*	harbour **le port** *luh por*
lake **le lac** *luh lak*	market **le marché** *luh mar'shay*
river **la rivière** *la reev'yair*	shopping centre / mall **le centre commercial** *luh soñtr ko'mairs'yal*
stadium **le stade** *luh stad*	theatre **le théâtre** *luh tay'atr*

museum
le musée
luh moo'zay

park
le parc
luh park

tourist information office
l'office du tourisme
lof'ees doo too'rees'm

town centre
centre ville
luh soñtr veel

train station
la gare
la gar

zoo
le zoo
luh zoo

Could you show me on the map?

Est-ce que vous pourriez me montrer sur la carte?

ess kuh voo poo'ree'ay muh mon'tray sur la kart

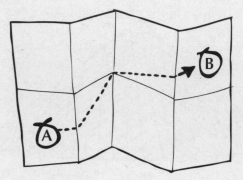

When does it open / close?

Ça ouvre / ferme à quelle heure?

sa oovr / fairm a kel uhr

Is there an entrance fee?

Est-ce qu'il faut payer l'entrée?

ess keel foh pay'ay lon'tray

Is there a discount for children / pensioners / students?
Y a-t-il une réduction pour les enfants / personnes âgées / etudiants?
ee a teel oon ray'dooks'yoñ poor layz on'foñ / pair'son a'zhay / ay'tood'yoñ

POSSIBLE REPLY
It's free.
C'est gratuit.
say grat'wee

Where do I pay?
Où est-ce que je peux payer?
oo ess kuh zhuh puh pay'ay

Is there wheelchair access?
Y a-t-il un accès handicapé?
ee a teel uñ ak'say oñ'dee'ka'pay

6

Are there disabled toilets?
Y a-t-il des toilettes pour handicapés?
ee a teel day twa'let poor oñ'dee'kap'ay

Would you take a photo of me / us, please?
Pouvez-vous prendre une photo de moi /
   nous, s'il vous plaît?
poo'vay voo prondr oon photo duh mwa /
   noo seel voo play

POSSIBLE REPLIES

Take the first / second / third turning on the
   left / right.
Prenez la première / deuxième / troisième
   rue à gauche / droite.
pruh'nay la pruhm'yair / duhz'yem /
   trwaz'yem roo a gohsh / drwat

Go straight on.
Allez tout droit.
a'lay too drwa

Around the corner.
C'est au coin de la rue.
say toh kwañ duh la roo

Along the street / road / avenue.
Le long de cette rue / route / avenue.
luh loñ duh set roo / root / av'noo

Over the bridge.
Traversez le pont.
tra'vair'say luh poñ

It's a ten-minute walk down that road.
C'est à dix minutes de marche par cette route.
say ta dee mee'noot duh marsh par set root

7

SPEND, SPEND, SPEND

SHOPPING

Open
Ouvert
oo'vair

Closed
Fermé
fair'may

Entrance
Entrée
añ'tray

Exit
Sortie
sor'tee

Where's the main shopping centre?
Où est le principal centre commercial?
oo ay luh prañ'see'pal soñtr ko'mairs'yal

Where can I find a … ?
Où est-ce que je peux trouver … ?
oo ess kuh zhuh puh troo'vay

baker's
la boulangerie
la boo'loñzh'ree

bookshop
la librairie
la lee'bray'ree

bank
la banque
la boñk

butcher's
le boucher
luh boo'shay

chemist's
la pharmacie

la far'ma'see

clothes shop
**le magasin de
    vêtements**
*luh ma'ga'zañ duh
    vet'moñ*

delicatessen
le traiteur
luh tray'tuhr

department store
le grand magasin
luh groñ ma'ga'zañ

fishmonger's
le poissonnier
luh pwa'son'yay

gift shop
le magasin de cadeaux
*luh ma'ga'zañ duh
    ka'doh*

greengrocer's
l'épicerie
lay'pees'ree

newsagent's
la presse
la press

post office
la poste
la posst

shoe shop
le magasin de chaussures
luh ma'ga'zañ duh shoh'soor

supermarket
le supermarché
luh soo'pair' marsh'ay

wine merchant
le marchant de vin
luh marsh'oñ duh vañ

How much is it?
Combien ça coûte?
kom'byañ sa koot

I'm just looking, thanks.
Je ne fais que regarder, merci.
zhuh ne fay kuh ruh'gar'day mair'see

Where are the changing rooms?
Où sont les cabines d'essayage?
oo soñ lay kab'eens de'say'azh

Excuse me, do you sell … ?
Excusez-moi, vendez-vous … ?
eks'koo'zay mwa voñ'day voo

alcohol
de l'alcool
duh lal'kol

aspirin
de l'aspirine
duh las'pee'reen

cigarettes
des cigarettes
day see'ga'ret

condoms
des préservatifs
day pray'sair'va'teef

postcards
des carte postales
day kart pos'tal

stamps
des timbres
day tañbr

English newspapers
des journaux anglais
day zhoor'noh oñ'glay

street maps of the local area
des plans des alentours
day ploñ dayz a'loñ'toor

I'll take one / two / three of those.
Je vais en prendre un / deux / trois.
zhuh vayz oñ proñdr uñ / duh / trwa

I'll take it.
Je vais le prendre.
zhuh vay luh proñdr

That's too expensive. Do you have anything
  cheaper?
**C'est trop cher. Avez-vous quelque chose de
  moins cher?**
*say troh shair. a'vay voo kel'kuh shohz duh
  mwañ shair*

7

Where do I pay?
Où est-ce que je peux payer?
oo ess kuh zhuh puh pay'ay

POSSIBLE REPLY
You can pay over there.
Vous pouvez payer là bas.
voo poo'vay pay'ay la bah

Could I have a bag, please?
Est-ce que je peux avoir un sac, s'il vous plaît?
ess kuh zhuh puhz a'vwar uñ sak seel voo play

I don't need a bag.
Je n'ai pas besoin d'un sac.
zhuh nay pah buhz'wañ duñ sak

POSSIBLE REPLIES

Can I help you?
Est-ce que je peux vous aider?
ess kuh zhuh puh vooz ay'day

We don't sell …
Nous ne vendons pas de …
noo nuh voñ'doñ pah duh

That'll be … euros, please.
Cela vous fera … euros, s'il vous plaît.
suh'la voo fuh'ra … uh'roh seel voo play

7

8 MEETING & GREETING

MAKING FRIENDS

Hi! My name is …
Salut! Je m'appelle …
sa'loo. zhuh ma'pel

Pleased to meet you.
Heureux(se) de faire ta / votre connaissance.
uhr'ruh(ruhze) duh fair ta / votr kon'ay'soñs

What's your name?
Comment vous appelez-vous?
ko'moñ vooz a'play voo

Where are you from?
D'où venez-vous?
doo vuh'nay voo

I'm from England
Je viens d'Angleterre.
zhuh vyañ doñ'gluh'tair

Have you been here long?
Etes-vous arrivé il y a longtemps?
et vooz a'ree'vay eel ee a loñ'toñ

How long are you here for?
Vous êtes ici pour combien de temps?
vooz et ee'see poor kom'byañ duh toñ

POSSIBLE REPLIES
I've just arrived.
Je viens d'arriver.
zhuh vyañ da'ree'vay

I've been here for … days / weeks / months.
J'y suis depuis … jours / semaines / mois
zhee swee duh'pwee … zhoor / suh'men / mwa

I live here.
J'habite ici.
zha'beet ee'see

How are you doing?
Comment allez-vous?
ko'moñ ta'lay voo

Fine, thanks. And you?
Bien, merci. Et vous?
byañ mair'see. ay voo

What do you do? [employment]
Que faites-vous dans la vie?
kuh fet voo doñ la vee

Would you like a drink?
Voudriez-vous boire quelque chose?
voo'dree'ay voo bwar kel'kuh shohz

Two beers, please.
Deux bières, s'il vous plaît.
duh byair seel voo play

It's my round.
C'est ma tourné(e).
say ma toor'nay

My friend is paying.
C'est mon ami qui paye.
say mon a'mee kee pay

Can we split the bill?
Est-ce que nous pouvons diviser l'addition?
ess kuh noo poo'voñ dee'vee'zay la'dees'yoñ

What's your friend's name?
Comment s'appelle votre ami(e)?
ko'moñ sa'pel votr a'mee

Are you single / married?
Etes-vous célibataire / marié(e)?
et voo say'lee'ba'tair / ma'ree'ay

Do you have a boyfriend / girlfriend?
Est-ce que vous avez un copain / une copine?
ess kuh vooz a'vay uñ ko'pañ / oon ko'peen

POSSIBLE REPLY
I have a boyfriend / girlfriend back home.
J'ai un copain / une copine chez moi.
zhay uñ ko'pañ / oon ko'peen shay mwa

Are you waiting for someone?
Attendez-vous quelqu'un?
a'toñ'day voo kel'kuñ

8

Do you want to dance?
Voulez-vous dancer?
voo'lay voo doñ'say

POSSIBLE REPLY
I'd love to, thanks.
Cela ma ferait très plaisir, merci.
suh'la muh fuh'ray tray play'zeer mair'see

What are you doing tomorrow?
Qu'est-ce que tu fais demain?
kess'kuh too fay duh'mañ

Are you free this weekend?
Est-ce que vous êtes libre ce weekend?
ess kuh vooz et leebr suh weekend

Would you like to have dinner with me?
Voulez-vous dîner avec moi?
voo'lay voo dee'nay a'vek mwa

Can I have your phone number /
  e-mail address?
**Pourrais-je avoir votre numéro de téléphone /
  adresse e-mail?**
*poo'rayzh a'vwar votr noo'may'roh duh
  tay'lay'fon / a'dress ee'mayl*

Here's my phone number. Call me some time.
**Voici mon numéro de téléphone. Appelez-
  moi à l'occasion.**
*vwa'see moñ noo'may'roh duh te'le'fon.
  ap'lay mwa a lo'kaz'yon*

What time shall we meet?
**A quelle heure voulez-vous que l'on se
  rencontre?**
*a kel uhr voo'lay voos kuh loñ suh
  ron'koñtr*

Let's meet at …
Nous pouvons nous rencontrer à …
noo poo'voñ noo ron'koñ'tray a

POSSIBLE REPLIES

Sorry, I'm with someone.
Desolé(e), je suis avec quelqu'un.
day'zo'lay zhuh sweez a'vek kel'kuñ

I've had a great evening.
J'ai passé une soirée très agreeable.
zhay pass'ay oon swa'ray trayz ag'ray'arbl

Leave me alone.
Laissez moi tranquille.
less'ay mwa troñ'keel

Sorry, you're not my type.
Desolé(e), vous n'êtes pas mon type.
day'zo'lay voo net pa moñ teep

9 EMERGENCIES

Call the police!
Appelez la police!
a'play la po'lees

Help!
A l'aide!
a led

My purse / wallet / bag / passport / mobile
phone has been stolen.
**Mon porte-monnaie / portefeuille / sac /
passeport / téléphone portable a été volé.**
*moñ port'mo'nay / port'foy / sak / pass'por /
tay'lay'fon por'tabl a aytay vo'lay*

Stop, thief!
Au voleur!
oh vo'luhr

Where's the police station?
Où est le commissariat?
oo ay luh ko'mee'sa'ree'a

Look out!   Fire!
Attention!   **Au feu!**
a'toñs'yoñ   *oh fuh*

Where's the emergency exit?
Où est l'issue de secours?
oo ay lee'soo duh suh'koor

Where's the hospital?
Où est l'hôpital?
oo ay lo'pee'tal

I feel ill.
Je me sens malade.
zhuh muh soñ mal'ad

I'm going to be sick.
Je vais vomir.
zhuh vay vo'meer

I've a terrible headache.
J'ai un terrible mal de tête.
zhay uñ tair'eebl mal duh tet

It hurts here … [point]
Ça me fait mal ici.
sa muh fay mal ee'see

Please call for a doctor / ambulance.
**Appelez un docteur / une ambulance, s'il
vous plaît.**
*a'play uñ dok'tuhr / oon oñ'boo'loñs seel
voo play*

Can you recommend an English-speaking
doctor / dentist?
**Pouvez-vous me recommander un medecin /
dentiste anglophone?**
*poo vay voo muh ruh'ko'moñ'day uñ
med'sañ / don'teest oñ'glo'fon*

I'm taking this prescription medication.
Je prends ce médicament sur prescription.
zhuh proñ suh may'dee'ka'moñ sur
  pruh'skreeps'yoñ

I'm pregnant.
Je suis enceinte.
zhuh sweez oñ'sañt

I'm allergic to …
Je suis allergique à …
zhuh sweez a'lair'zheek a

I'm lost. Can you help me?
Je me suis perdu(e). Pouvez-vous m'aider?
zhuh muh swee pair'doo. poo'vay voo
  may'day

10 REFERENCE

NUMBERS

0 zero
zéro
zay'roh

1 one
un
uñ

2 two
deux
duh

3 three
trois
trwa

4 four
quatre
katr

5 five
cinq
sañk

6 six
six
sees

7 seven
sept
set

8	eight	14	fourteen
	huit		**quatorze**
	weet		*ka'torz*

9	nine	15	fifteen
	neuf		**quinze**
	nuhf		*kañz*

10	ten	16	sixteen
	dix		**seize**
	dees		*sez*

11	eleven	17	seventeen
	onze		**dix-sept**
	oñz		*dee'set*

12	twelve	18	eighteen
	douze		**dix-huit**
	dooz		*deez'weet*

13	thirteen	19	nineteen
	treize		**dix-neuf**
	trez		*deez'nuhf*

20	twenty **vingt** *vañ*		**40**	forty **quarante** *ka′roñt*
21	twenty-one **vingt et un** *vañ′tay′uñ*		**41**	forty-one **quarante et un** *ka′roñ′tay′uñ*
22	twenty-two **vingt-deux** *vañ′duh*		**42**	forty-two **quarante-deux** *ka′roñt′duh*
30	thirty **trente** *troñt*		**50**	fifty **cinquante** *sañ′koñt*
31	thirty-one **trente et un** *troñ′tay′un*		**60**	sixty **soixante** *swa′soñt*
32	thirty-two **trente-deux** *troñt′duh*		**70**	seventy **soixante-dix** *swa′soñt′dees*

REFERENCE

80 eighty
quatre-vingts
katr´vañ

90 ninety
quatre-vingt-dix
katr´vañ´dees

100 one hundred
cent
soñ

101 one hundred
and one
cent et un
soñ´tay´uñ

150 one hundred
and fifty
cent-cinquante
soñ sañ´koñt

200 two hundred
deux cents
duh soñ

500 five hundred
cinq cents
sañk soñ

1,000
one thousand
mille
meel

5,000
five thousand
cinq mille
sañk meel

1,000,000
one million
un million
uñ meel´yoñ

DAYS OF THE WEEK

Monday
lundi
luñ'dee

Saturday
samedi
sam'dee

Tuesday
mardi
mar'dee

Sunday
dimanche
dee'moñsh

Wednesday
mercredi
mair'kruh'dee

Thursday
jeudi
zhuh'dee

Friday
vendredi
voñ'druh'dee

REFERENCE

MONTHS OF THE YEAR

January
janvier
zhoñ'vee'ay

February
février
fay'vree'ay

March
mars
marss

April
avril
a'vreel

May
mai
may

June
juin
zhoo'añ

July
juillet
zhoo'ee'ay

August
août
oo

September
septembre
sep'toñbr

October
octobre
oc'tobr

November
novembre
noh'voñbr

December
decembre
day'soñbr

TIMES OF DAY

today
aujourd'hui
oh'zhoor'dwee

tomorrow
demain
duh'mañ

yesterday
hier
ee'air

the day after
  tomorrow
le lendemain
luh loñ'duh'mañ

morning
le matin
luh ma'tañ

afternoon
l'apres-midi
la'pray mee'dee

evening
le soir
luh swar

now
maintenant
mañ'te'noñ

later
plus tard
ploo tar

10

REFERENCE

TIME

Excuse me. What's the time?
Excusez-moi. Quelle heure est-il?
eks'koo'zay mwa. kel uhr ay'teel

It's one o'clock.
Il est une heure.
eel ayt oon uhr

It's quarter to eight.
Il est huit heures moins le quart.
eel ay weet uhr mwañ luh kar

It's half past two.
Il est deux heures et demi.
eel ay duhz uhr ay duh'mee

It's quarter past ten.
Il est dix heures et quart.
eel ay deez uhr ay kar

Five past seven.
Sept heure cinq.
set uhr sañk

Ten past eleven
Onze heures dix
oñz uhr dees

Ten to five.
Cinq heures moins dix.
sañk uhr mwañ dees

Twelve o'clock (noon / midnight)
Midi / minuit
mee'dee / mee'nwee

KEY VOCABULARY

Please note, an (*m*), masculine,(*f*), feminine, or
(*pl*), plural, after a noun denotes its gender.

A

accept	**accepter**
access	**accéder (à)**
address	**adresse** (*f*)
afternoon	**après-midi**
ahead	**devant**
after	**après**
after-dinner drink	**digestif** (*m*)
airport	**l'aéroport** (*m*)
air-conditioning	**la climatisation**
aisle	**couloir** (*m*)
allow	**permettre**
along	**le long de**
alcohol	**l'alcool**
allergic	**allergique (à)**
alone	**tout seul**
ambulance	**ambulance** (*f*)
another	**un(e) autre**
appetizer	**un apéritif**

April	**avril**
area	**région** (f)
around	**vers**
arrive	**arriver**
art gallery	**galerie d'art** (f)
aspirin	**aspirine** (f)
August	**aôut**
avenue	**avenue** (f)
avoid	**éviter**

B

back (adv.)	**en arrière**
bad	**mauvais**
bag	**sac** (m)
baggage	**bagages** (pl)
baker	**boulangerie** (f)
balcony	**balcon** (m)
bank	**banque** (f)
bar	**bar** (m)
barbecue	**barbecue** (m)
bath	**bain** (m)
(to) be	**être**
beach	**plage** (f)
bed	**lit** (m)
before	**avant**

behind	**derrière**
beverage	**boisson** (f)
bicycle	**vélo** (m)
bill	**addition** (f)
boarding pass	**carte d'embarquement** (f)
boat	**bâteau** (m)
book (v.)	**réserver**
bookshop	**librairie** (f)
bottle	**bouteille** (f)
boy	**garçon** (m)
boyfriend	**copain** (m)
breakfast	**petit déjeuner** (m)
bridge	**pont** (m)
brunch	**brunch** (m)
bus	**bus** (m)
butcher's	**boucherie** (f)
buy	**acheter**
by (near)	**à côté de**

C

call (n.; v.)	**appel; appeler**
camp (v.)	**faire du camping**
can (v.)	**pouvoir**
car	**voiture** (f)
caravan	**caravane** (f)

cash	**espèces** (*fpl*)
cash machine	**distributeur d'argent** (*m*)
castle	**château** (*m*)
catch	**prendre (un bus / train)**
cathedral	**cathédral** (*f*)
change (*v.*)	**changer**
changing rooms	**cabines d'essayage** (*pl*)
charge (*n.; v.*)	**tarif / frais / charges** (*mpl*); **facturer**
cheap(er)	**bon marché/moins cher; pas cher**
checkout (*n.*)	*see* till
check out (*v.*)	**libérer (une chambre); quitter (un hotel)**
chemist's	**pharmacie** (*f*)
children	**enfants** (*mpl*)
cigarettes	**cigarettes** (*pl*)
cinema	**cinéma** (*m*)
clean (*v.; adj.*)	**nettoyer; propre**
close/d	**fermer / fermé(e)**
clothes	**vêtements** (*pl*)
clothes shop	**magasin de vêtements** (*m*)
code	**mot de passe** (*m*)
coeliac	**cœliaque**
cold	**froid**

commission	**commission** (*f*)
complaint	**plainte** (*f*)
condiment	**condiment** (*m*)
condoms	**préservatifs** (*pl*)
contain	**contenir**
cook	**cuisiner**
corner	**coin** (*m*)
cost (*n.; v.*)	**frais** (*m*)**; couter**
couple	**couple** (*m*)
credit card	**carte de crédit** (*f*)
currency	
exchange office	**bureau de change** (*m*)
current	**actuel**

D

dairy	**produits laitiers** (*pl*)
dance (*v.*)	**danser**
day	**jour** (*m*)
December	**décembre**
departure lounge	**salle d'embarquement** (*f*)
delicatessen	**épicerie** (*f*)
delicious	**délicieux**
dentist	**dentiste** (*f*)
deodorant	**déodorant** (*m*)
department store	**grand magasin** (*m*)

dessert	**dessert** (*m*)
diesel	**diesel / gasoil** (*m*)
dining room	**salle à manger** (*f*)
dinner	**dîner** (*m*)
to have dinner	**prendre le dîner**
dirty	**sale**
disabled	**handicapé(e)**
discount	**réduction** (*f*)
dish	**plat** (*m*)
do	**faire**
do not	**ne … pas …**
doctor	**médecin** (*m*)
double	**double**
down	**en bas**
drink (*n.; v.*)	**boisson** (*f*)**; boire**
to have a drink	**prendre un verre**

E

eat	**manger**
electricity	**électricité** (*f*)
e-mail	**email** (*m*)
emergency	**secours** (*m*)
England	**Angleterre**
English	**anglais**
English-speaking	**anglophone**

enjoy	**amuser**
enter	**entrer**
entrance	**entrée** (*f*)
evening	**soir** (*m*)
exchange	**échange**
excuse me	**excusez-moi**
exit	**sortie** (*f*)
expensive	**cher**

F

fare	**tarif**
February	**février**
fee	**tarif** (*m*)
feel	**sentir**
ferry	**ferry** (*m*)
find / found	**trouver / trouvé(e)**
fine (money)	**amende** (*f*)
fine (well/ok)	**bien**
fire!	**feu!**
first	**premier**
fish	**poisson** (*f*)
fishmonger's	**poissonnière** (*f*)
follow	**suivre**
food	**nourriture** (*f*)
for	**pour**

fork	**fourchette** (f)
free (*adj.*)	**gratuit**
freezer	**congélateur** (m)
fresh	**frais**
Friday	**vendredi**
fridge	**réfrigérateur** (m)
friend	**ami(e)** (m/f)
from	**de**
frozen	**gelé**
fruit	**fruit**
full	**rempli**

G

gate	**porte** (f) **(d'embarquement)**
gift shop	**boutique de cadeaux** (f)
girl	**fille** (f)
girlfriend	**copine** (f)
glass	**verre** (m)
go	**aller**
good	**bon**
goodbye	**au revoir**
grams	**grammes**
great	**super**
greengrocer	**l'épicerie** (f)

H

hairdryer	**sèche-cheveux** (*m*)
half	**demi**
handful	**poignée** (*f*)
harbour	**port** (*m*)
have (infin.)	**avoir**
headache	**avoir mal à la tête**
hello	**bonjour**
help	**aide**
here	**ici**
hi	**salut**
hire	**louer**
home	**à la maison**
hospital	**hôpital** (*m*)
hostel	**auberge de jeunesse** (*f*)
hot	**chaud(e)**
hotel	**hôtel**
hour	**heure**
how	**comment**
how far	**à quelle distance**
how many	**combien**
how much (cost)	**c'est combien / combien coûte**
hundred	**cent**
hungry	**avoir faim**

hurt	**blessé**
husband	**mari** (m)

I

I am	**je suis**
ill	**malade**
in	**dans**
in front of	**devant**
include	**inclure**
information	**renseignements** (f)
it's	**c'est**
item	**article** (m)

J

January	**janvier**
July	**juillet**
June	**juin**
just	**juste**

K

key	**clé** (m)
kilogram	**kilogramme** (m)
kitchen	**cuisine** (f)
knife	**couteau** (m)

L

ladies	**femmes** (*fpl*)
lake	**lac** (*m*)
last	**dernier**
late	**tard**
later	**plus tard**
leave	**partir**
left (direction)	**gauche**
less	**moins**
like (*v.*)	**aimer**
live	**vivre**
local (*adj.*)	**de la région**
local area	**région** (*f*)
long (time)	**longtemps**
look	**regarder**
look out!	**attention!**
lost	**perdu(e)**
love (*v.*)	**aimer; adorer**
luggage	**bagages** (*mpl*)
lunch	**déjeuner** (*m*)

M

make	**faire**
main	**principal(e)**
main course	**plat principal**

mall	**centre commercial** (m)
map	**carte** (f)
market	**marché** (m)
married	**marié**
may I / we	**est-ce que je pourrais / nous pourrions**
May	**mai**
me	**moi**
meal	**repas** (m)
meat	**viande** (f)
medication	**médicaments** (pl)
meeting place	**rendez-vous**
menu	**menu** (m)
midday	**midi**
midnight	**minuit**
million	**million**
mini-bar	**mini bar** (m)
minutes	**minutes**
mistake	**erreur** (f)
mobile	**phone portable** (m)
moment	**moment** (m)
Monday	**lundi**
month	**mois**
more	**plus**
morning	**matin**

museum	**musée** (*m*)
my	**mon / ma / mes**

N

name	**nom**
near	**près de**
nearest	**plus proche**
nearby	**près**
need	**avoir besoin de**
news	**nouvelles**
newsagent	**tabac** (*m*)
newspaper	**journal** (*m*)
next	**prochain(e)**
night	**nuit** (*f*)
night club	**boite (de nuit)** (*f*)
noisy	**bruyant**
not	**pas**
November	**novembre**
now	**maintenant**
number	**numéro**

O

October	**octobre**
of	**de**
on	**sur**

open (*adj.*)	**ouvert(e)**
opposite	**en face de**
order (*n.; v.*)	**commande** (*f*); **commander**
our	**notre / nos**
out of	**dehors**
outside	**dehors**
over there	**par là**

P

pardon	**pardon**
park (*n.; v.*)	**parc** (*m*)**; garer**
passport	**passeport** (*m*)
pay	**payer**
people	**gens**
pensioner	**personne âgée**
per	**par (par personne)**
person	**personne**
pet	**animal domestique** (*m*)
petrol	**essence** (*f*)
phone (*n.; v.*)	**téléphone** (*m*)**; appeler**
photo (*n.; v.*)	**photo** (*f*)**; prendre une photo**
place	**endroit** (*m*)
platform	**voie** (*m*)

please	**s'il vous plaît**
(to be) pleased	**c'est un plaisir de ...**
police	**police** (f)
police station	**commissariat** (f)
pool	**piscine** (f)
pop	*see* soft drink
postcard	**carte postale** (f)
post office	**bureau de poste** (m)
pregnant	**enceinte**
prescription	**ordonnance**
print (v.)	**imprimer**
porter	**bagagiste** (m)
pound	
(currency; weight)	**livre** (f)
price	**prix** (m)
public	**public**
purse	**porte-monnaie** (m)

Q

| quarter | **quart** |

R

radio	**radio** (m)
rate (n.)	**taux** (m)
ready	**prête**

reception	**réception** (f)
recommend	**recommander**
red	**rouge**
reduction	**réduction** (f)
reserve	**réserver**
restaurant	**restaurant** (m)
return	**retourner**
right (direction)	**à droite**
river	**rivière** (f)
road	**route** (f)
room	**chambre** (f)

S

safe (n.)	**le coffre-fort** (m)
salad	**salade** (f)
satisfy	**satisfaire**
Saturday	**samedi**
seat	**siège** (f)
second	**deuxième**
section	**partie**
sell	**vendre**
September	**septembre**
serve	**servir**
service	**service** (m)
shampoo	**shampooing** (m)

shaving foam	**mousse à raser** (*m*)
shoe shop	**magasin de chaussures** (*m*)
shop	**magasin** (*m*)
shopping centre	**centre commercial** (*m*)
show (*n.; v.*)	**spectacle** (*m*)**; montrer**
shower	**douche** (*m*)
shower gel	**gel douche** (*m*)
sick	**malade**
sign	**panneau** (*m*)
similar	**similaire**
sing	**chanter**
single	**célibataire**
slice(s)	**tranche(s)**
small	**petit(e)**
smoked	**fumé**
snack (*v.*)	**grignote**
soap	**savon** (*m*)
soft drink	**boisson sans alcool** (*m*)
some	**quelque**
someone	**quelqu'un**
something	**quelque chose**
sorry	**désolé**
split	**diviser**
spoon	**cuillère** (*f*)
stadium	**stade** (*m*)

stairs	**escaliers** (*pl*)
stamps	**timbres** (*pl*)
station	**gare** (*f*)
stay	**rester**
stock	**stock** (*m*)
stolen	**volé**
stop	**arrêter**
straight	**direct / tout droit**
street	**rue** (*f*)
street map	**plan de ville** (*m*)
student	**étudiant(e)** (*m/f*)
suitcase	**valise** (*f*)
Sunday	**dimanche**
supermarket	**supermarché** (*m*)
supply	**fournir**
swimming	**natation** (*f*)

T

table	**table** (*f*)
take	**prendre**
taxi	**taxi** (*m*)
telephone	**téléphone/portable** (*m*) (mobile)
television	**télévision** (*f*)
tell	**dire**

ten	**dix**
tent	**tente** (*m*)
terminal	**terminale** (*f*)
terrace	**terrasse**
terrible	**terrible**
thanks	**merci**
theatre	**théâtre** (*f*)
there	**là**
thief	**voleur**
third	**troisième**
thirsty	**avoir soif**
thousand	**mille**
Thursday	**jeudi**
ticket	**ticket / billet** (*m*)
till	**caisse** (*f*)
time	**l'heure**
to	**à**
today	**aujourd'hui**
toilets	**toilettes** (*fpl*)
toiletries	**articles de toilette** (*mpl*)
tomorrow	**demain**
toothbrush	**brosse à dents** (*f*)
toothpaste	**dentifrice**
tourist information office	**office de tourisme** (*m*)

towel	**serviette** (*f*)
town	**ville** (*m*)
town centre	**centre-ville** (*m*)
train	**train** (*m*)
train station	**gare** (*f*)
tram	**tramway** (*m*)
traveller's cheques	**chèques de voyage** (*pl*)
treat	**cadeau** (*m*)
Tuesday	**mardi**
turning	**embranchement;**
	carrefour (*m*)
twin	**jumeau / jumelle**
type	**type** (*m*)

U

unleaded	**sans plomb**
up	**en haut**

V

vacancy(ies)	**chambre(s) libre(s)**
vegan	**végétalien(ne)**
vegetarian	**végétarien(ne)**
view	**vue**

W

wait	**attendre**
waiter	**serveur**
waitress	**serveuse**
wake-up call	**réveil téléphonique** (m)
walk	**promenade** (f)
wallet	**portefeuille** (m)
want	**vouloir**
washing-up liquid	**liquide vaisselle** (m)
water (still / sparkling)	**eau minérale/ eau gazeuse** (f)
Wednesday	**mecredi**
week	**semaine** (f)
weekend	**weekend** (m)
welcome	**bienvenue**
well	**bien**
what	**quel(le)**
wheelchair	**fauteuil roulant** (m)
when	**quand**
where (is / are)	**où (est / sont)**
which	**quel(le)**
white	**blanc(he)**
who	**qui**
wife	**femme** (f)
Wi-Fi	**wifi** (m)

window	**fenêtre** (*f*)
wine	**vin** (*m*)
with	**avec**
work	**travail** (*m*)
why	**pourquoi**

Y

you	**vous/tu**
year	**année**
yesterday	**hier**

Z

| zoo | **zoo** (*m*) |

FOOD

anchovy	**anchois** (*m*)
aubergine	**aubergine** (*f*)
bacon	**bacon** (*m*)
beans	**haricots** (*mpl*)
beef	**boeuf** (*m*)
biscuit	**biscuit** (*m*)
bread	**pain** (*m*)
cake	**gâteau** (*m*)
chicken	**poulet** (*m*)
chips	*see* fries

chocolate	**chocolat** (m)
chocolate mousse	**mousse au chocolat** (f)
cookie	**cookie** (m)
courgette	**courgette** (f)
crisps	**chips** (fpl)
custard	**crème anglaise** (f)

DAIRY

butter	**beurre** (m)
cheese	**fromage** (m)
cream	**crème** (f)
cream cheese	**fromage frais** (m)
egg	**oeuf** (m)
yoghurt	**yaourt** (m)

fillet	**filet** (m)
fish	**poisson** (f)
flan	**flan** (m)
flour	**farine** (f)
fries	**frites** (fpl)

FRUIT

apple	**pomme** (f)
apricot	**abricot** (m)
banana	**banane** (f)

blackberry	**mûre** (*f*)
blueberry	**myrtille** (*m*)
cherry	**cerise** (*f*)
cranberry	**canneberge** (*f*)
grape	**raisin** (*m*)
grapefruit	**pamplemousse** (*m*)
lemon	**citron** (*m*)
lime	**citron vert** (*m*)
mango	**mangue** (*f*)
orange	**orange** (*m*)
passion fruit	**fruit de la passion** (*m*)
peach	**pêche** (*f*)
pear	**poire** (*f*)
pineapple	**ananas** (*m*)
plum	**prune** (*f*)
pomegranate	**grenade** (*f*)
raspberry	**framboise** (*f*)
strawberry	**fraise** (*f*)
watermelon	**pastèque** (*f*)

gammon	**jambon** (*m*)
gravy	**sauce** (*f*)
ham	**jambon** (*m*)

ice cream	**glace** (f)
lamb	**agneau** (m)
minced meat	**viande hachée** (f)
mustard	**moutarde** (f)
noodles	**nouilles** (fpl)
nuts	**noix** (mpl)
olives	**olives** (f)
olive oil	**huile d'olives** (f)
pasta	**patés** (m)
pepper (seasoning)	**poivre** (m)
pie	**tarte** (f)
pork	**porc** (m)
rabbit	**lapin** (f)
rice	**riz** (m)
roast beef	**rosbif** (m)
rump	**rumsteck** (m)
salad	**salade** (f)
salt	**sel** (m)
sauce	**sauce** (fpl)
sausage(s)	**saucisson** (m) / **saucisses** (fpl)
sirloin	**aloyau** (m)
snail	**escargot** (m)
soup	**potage** (m)
steak	**steak** (m)

toast	**toast** (m)
tomato ketchup	**ketchup** (m)
turkey	**dinde** (f)

VEGETABLES	**légumes** (mpl)
artichoke	**artichaut** (m)
asparagus	**asperge** (f)
broccoli	**brocoli** (m)
carrot	**carrotte** (f)
cauliflower	**chou-fleur** (m)
celery	**céler** (m)
corn	**maïs** (m)
courgette	**courgette** (f)
cucumber	**concombre** (m)
eggplant	**aubergine** (f)
lettuce	**salade** (f)
mushroom	**champignon** (m)
onion	**onion** (m)
peas	**petit pois** (m)
pepper (vegetable)	**poivron** (m)
potato	**pomme de terre** (f)
radish	**radis** (m)
spinach	**épinard** (m)
tomato	**tomate** (f)

vanilla	**vanille** (*f*)
veal	**veau** (*m*)
venison	**venaison** (*f*)
vinegar	**vinaigre** (*m*)
wheat	**blé** (*m*)

DRINK

apple juice	**jus de pomme** (*m*)
alcohol	**alcool** (*m*)
beer	**bière** (*f*)
champagne	**champagne** (*m*)
cider	**cidre** (*m*)
cocktail	**cocktail** (*m*)
coffee	**café** (*m*)
cola	**coca** (*m*)
espresso	**espresso** (*m*)
gin and tonic	**gin tonic** (*m*)
hot chocolate	**chocolat chaud** (*m*)
iced tea	**icetea** (*m*)
juice	**jus** (*m*)
lager	**bière blonde** (*f*)
lemonade	**limonade** (*f*)
milk	**lait** (*m*)
orange juice	**jus d'orange** (*m*)
red wine	**vin rouge** (*m*)

rosé wine	**vin rose** (*m*)
soda	**soda** (*m*)
sparkling water	**eau gazeuse** (*f*)
still mineral water	**eau minéral** (*f*)
tap water	**eau robinet** (*f*)
tea	**thé** (*m*)
black tea	**thé nature** (*m*)
herbal	**infusion** (*f*)
white wine	**vin blanc** (*m*)